BOOKS IN THIS SERIES

BETTER TENNIS

FOR BOYS AND GIRLS

GEORGE SULLIVAN

Illustrated with photographs

DODD, MEAD & COMPANY
New York

Distributed in Canada by
McClelland and Stewart Limited, Toronto
Manufactured in the United States of America

1 2 3 4 5 6 7 8 9 10

Library of Congress Cataloging-in-Publication Data

Sullivan, George, 1927–
Better tennis for boys and girls.

Summary: Discusses the rules, scoring, equipment,
techniques, and tactics of tennis.
1. Tennis—Juvenile literature. [1. Tennis]
I. Title.
GV996.5.S95 1987   796.342′2   86-29123
ISBN 0-396-08939-9

ACKNOWLEDGMENTS

The author is grateful to many individuals who cooperated with him in the preparation of this book. Special thanks are due Rich Bray, tennis professional at the Twin Hills Country Club, Longmeadow, Massachusetts, and to the boys and girls from Longmeadow and East Longmeadow who posed for the photos that appear in the book. They include Maria Cacciapouti, Josh Sifrin, Neela and Ravi Thakur, and Jeff and Scott Pothul. The author is also grateful to tennis pro Lloyd Lifton for checking portions of the manuscript; Herb Field, Herb Field Art Studio; Francesca Kurti, TLC Custom Labs; and Aime LaMontagne.

CONTENTS

A teaching pro will help you improve your game.

8

INTRODUCTION

Bill Tilden, who won six straight U.S. Singles Championships during the 1920s, and who is sometimes hailed as the best American player ever, once drew up a blueprint for tennis success. This was his advice:

1. Learn the correct racket grips.
2. Learn the correct footwork and body position.
3. Learn to hit the ball.
4. Learn to hit the ball correctly.
5. Learn to hit the ball correctly to a certain place.
6. Learn to hit the ball correctly to a certain place hard, slow, or at an even pace.

While tennis equipment and courts may have changed a great deal since Bill Tilden's day, the playing techniques have not. It's still a matter of learning the basics and knowing how to hit the ball correctly to a certain place at a certain speed.

As you can judge from this description, there is nothing mysterious about tennis. You can learn to play in a relatively short time if you want to work at it.

The game offers many benefits. Since it is vigorous exercise—during a three-set match, you'll run more than a mile—tennis will help to keep you physically fit. In terms of fitness, tennis is rivaled only by soccer and track.

And you keep gaining these benefits throughout your lifetime. Men and women in their fifties and sixties play tennis to help keep fit.

Another thing. Since tennis is a one-on-one sport, just you vs. a single opponent, you're often under pressure. This can help your sense of self-reliance, your confidence.

The sport also has social values. You'll make new friends at public courts in your neighborhood or at your local tennis club. You may want to play on your school team or, later, your college team. You can, in fact, play anywhere in the world because the rules are the same on every continent.

There are no shortcuts, however, in becoming a superior player, a junior champion. You begin by learning the basics and then progressing slowly through serious practice.

An instructor, a teaching pro, can help you to improve. You and your parents should investigate carefully before you choose a pro. You want someone who not only understands tennis strokes but who is an excellent teacher as well. Talk to other boys and girls who are taking lessons from the pro. Ask them what they're learning and whether they're enjoying it.

Once you become skilled, you may want to try tournament tennis. By playing in a tournament you'll learn how to concentrate under pressure. You'll learn good sportsmanship. Tournaments

also give you the opportunity to travel to other cities and meet new people.

Several organizations offer junior tennis competition. These include the National Public Parks Tennis Association, the American Tennis Association, and the United States Tennis Association, the USTA. (The USTA is the governing body of tennis in the United States.)

You may have first learned about tennis through the USTA's National Schools Program. The idea of the Schools Program is to teach tennis skills to students during school physical education classes.

The USTA also sponsors the National Junior Tennis League, which involves both instruction and competition on public courts.

The USTA is well known for its fully developed junior tournament program that produces champions in several age categories on both a sectional and national basis. If your family belongs to a tennis club, the club is likely to have a junior program that includes junior competition sponsored by the USTA.

For more information about these and other USTA programs for juniors, write the USTA Education and Research Center (720 Alexander Road, Princeton, NJ 08540).

Instruction in volleying at a New York City playground.

Stroke practice; you have to work hard to become a good player.

Learning to play tennis is something like learning to swim or bake a cake. Just about anyone can do it with the right instruction and determination to practice.

Just as some people become superior swimmers or bakers, so some become better tennis players than others. But just about everyone can at least learn how to get the ball back over the net.

The better you play, the greater the rewards. The important thing about tennis is to relax and have fun. Gritting your teeth, clenching your fists, or throwing your racket aren't going to help your game. A relaxed player almost always beats an angry one.

Whenever you go out onto the court, plan on having a good time. When you stop having fun, stop playing tennis.

HOW THE GAME IS PLAYED AND SCORED

The idea of tennis is simple: you hit the ball over the net and inside the court, and try to keep doing it longer than your opponent.

The rules are simple, too. They have been developing since the 1870s when the game was first played in England.

Actually, there are two kinds of tennis—singles and doubles. In singles, one player opposes another. In doubles, there are two players on a side. When each doubles team is made up of a man and woman, it's called mixed doubles.

Singles and doubles are played on the same court. It's rectangular in shape, divided by a net stretched across the middle. The net is 3 feet high at the center and 3½ feet high at the side posts to which it is attached.

View of the court showing alley on the right, center line and net and right post.

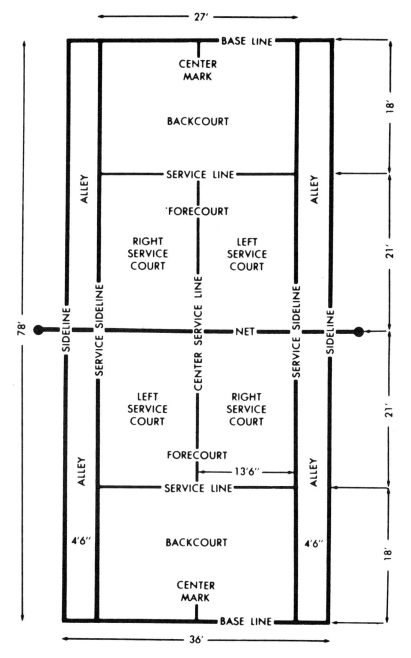

The court is 78 feet long. The court for singles is 27 feet wide. For doubles, an alley that is 4½ feet wide on each side of the court is put in use, making the court 36 feet wide.

Other lines divide the court into sections. The lines and the sections they form are shown on the court diagram here.

For almost a century, major tennis tournaments were played on grass courts. In fact, the early name for the sport was *lawn* tennis.

But grass courts cost too much to maintain. They have gone the way of free road maps and drugstores with soda fountains. Today, only one important tournament is contested on grass. That is the All-England Championships, played at Wimbledon, a suburb of London.

Tennis outdoors is now played on concrete, asphalt, clay, or a variety of synthetic surfaces. Indoor courts often have a synthetic surface laid down over wood or concrete.

The serve, or service, puts the ball in play. The server tosses the ball into the air and hits it before it strikes the ground. It must be hit into the service court diagonally opposite.

Once a legal serve has been made, the receiver must hit the ball on the first bounce and return it over the net. The only lines that count after that are the base lines and the sidelines. If the ball

White lines divide the court into different sections.

bounces on or within them, or is touched by a player before it bounces, it is in play. To keep the ball in play, the opponent must return it before it bounces more than once.

To many people, the scoring seems complicated. It's really not. But the terminology can cause problems. If you understand the meaning of the terms, scoring should not be difficult for you.

"Love" is one of those terms. Love means zero or nothing in tennis. Love is where you begin.

Tennis is scored in terms of points, games, and sets. A player scores a "point" when his or her opponent fails to make a legal return. Instead of naming the points 1, 2, 3, and 4, as in other sports, tennis has its own names:

- 1st point won by a player is called 15
- 2nd point won by a player is called 30
- 3rd point won by a player is called 40

The server's score is always given first. For example, if you are serving and lead three points to one, the score is 40-15. If your opponent wins the first two points when you are serving, the score is love-30.

When a player wins four points before his opponent wins three, he has won a "game." But if each player wins three points, the game is tied at 40-40, which is called "deuce," and the game continues until one player or the other gains a two-point advantage.

The first point scored after deuce is called "advantage" or "ad." If you have the advantage and lose the next point, the game returns to deuce.

To win a "set," one player must win six games before his opponent wins five. If the games are tied at 5-5—a deuce set—play continues until one player has a two-game margin.

Should the score reach 6-6, a tie breaker is used. A tie breaker is a playoff of a certain number of points. In one common tie breaker, the first player to win 5-out-of-9 points is the winner. Another method is based on 7-out-of-12 points. The player that wins the tie breaker wins by a score of 7-6.

In most junior tournaments, the first player to win two sets wins the "match."

These are the basic rules. For a complete rundown, write the Publications Division, U.S. Tennis Association (729 Alexander Road, Princeton, NJ 08540) and request the booklet titled *Rules of Tennis and Cases and Decisions*. It costs $2.25, which includes shipping and handling.

Besides what's been officially established, there are certain other rules of conduct you should follow. For example, it's your obligation to call all balls on your side of the net, announcing those that go out. You should also help your opponent to make calls when he or she requests help. Don't hesitate to call against yourself any ball that you clearly see out on your opponent's side of the net.

If you have any doubt as to whether a ball is in or out, you must give your opponent the benefit of the doubt and play the ball as good. If you call a ball out and then realize it was good, you should correct the call.

What's said above also applies to "let" balls. A let ball is any point that is played over because of interference of one type or another. The most common let is the let serve. In this, the ball touches the net before landing in the proper service court. The let serve does not count as a fault. The server simply serves again.

Any "out" or "let" call must be made immediately, that is, before you or your opponent hits the return or before the ball goes out of play. Otherwise, the ball remains in play.

To help avoid arguments over the score, the server should announce the set score—5-4, for example—before starting a game. And the game score—40-30, for example—should be announced by the server before serving a point.

YOUR EQUIPMENT

To play tennis, about all you need is a racket that enables you to hit the ball with power and control and a comfortable pair of shoes. Take your time in making your choices.

There are no rules that govern the size and weight of the racket. If you wanted to, you could use a Ping-Pong paddle or even a frying pan.

This means that there are many different shapes and styles of rackets from which to choose. The head size is very important. There are three types: traditional (the smallest), mid-size, and oversize.

The oversize racket gives you a very big hitting area (as much as 125 square inches). Many instructors believe that the oversize racket can be of real benefit to the beginner. "You feel you can't miss the ball," says one instructor. "The oversize racket builds confidence."

When buying a racket of this type, be sure to ask for a junior oversize. The word "junior" helps to assure that you'll get a racket that has the right grip size and is of the proper weight.

The weight is usually marked near the throat. (Racket parts are labeled in the diagram on next page.) A "heavy" racket is one that weighs from 14 to 15 ounces. A racket of this weight would be suitable for an adult or a very strong teenager.

A "medium" racket weighs from 13½ to 13¾

Hitting with an oversize racket (left) can help to build your confidence.

17

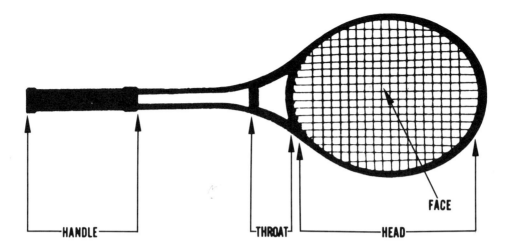

HANDLE   THROAT   HEAD   FACE

ounces, and a "light" racket from 12½ to 13 ounces.

Try rackets of different weights until you find one that seems suitable. (At some clubs, rackets can be rented.) A racket that is too light can be as troublesome as one that is too heavy. A light racket can twist in your hand as you stroke the ball, which makes for a poor hit. Another drawback is that it may cause you to put too much wrist action into your stroke. You want to hit with a firm wrist.

If you own a racket that seems too light, you can apply a strip of metallic tape to the frame to increase its weight. Ask a local tennis professional about such tape.

Racket frames used to be made of either wood or aluminum. But in recent years many other materials have become available. These include graphite, Kevlar, and boron. These materials, although light in weight, are very strong. They last longer than wood rackets but cost more.

There is also the matter of strings to consider. Most rackets are strung with nylon, some with gut. Nylon is the best for beginners because it's less expensive and doesn't require as much care as gut.

A racket can be expensive. They begin at around $50 and range up to $150. When making your selection, keep in mind that the best racket in the world won't make you a top-ranked player.

18

More important than the racket is how you hit the ball, your stroke-making ability. A racket of average cost should do fine.

Tennis shoes have composition or rubber soles and no heels. They not only help to keep you from slipping but are designed so as not to damage the court. Pick out shoes for comfort, not because of a particular side-striping or brand name.

Tennis balls, which are 2½ to 2⅝ inches in diameter, are hollow. Made of rubber, they are covered with a felt fabric of woven nylon, Dacron, and wool.

Whenever possible, use balls that are either new or close to new because they bounce better. Balls began to lose their liveliness the moment you open the sealed container. After two or three weeks, most balls no longer bounce well or give a good response when hit.

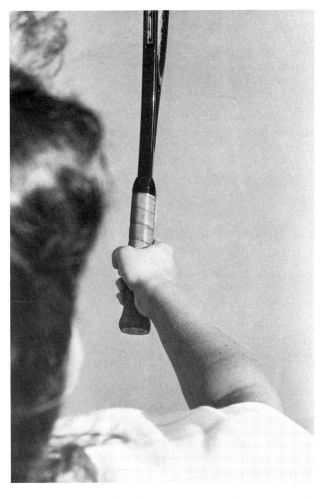

In the Eastern forehand grip, simply shake hands with the racket.

THE FOREHAND

The forehand is the most important of all the tennis strokes. Not only is it a basic weapon in your arsenal, but it also contains elements that are used in hitting the backhand and the serve.

THE READY POSITION—As you await the ball, you should be positioned so that you can move quickly and smoothly to your right or left, forward or back.

Grip the racket in your right hand and point it toward the net. Using the left hand, support the racket at the throat. This relieves the right hand of some of the racket's weight.

Your feet should be about shoulder-width apart. Bend your knees slightly. Your weight should be on the balls of your feet.

As your opponent gets set to swing, ease up onto your toes; get your heels off the ground. This helps you in pushing off in whatever direction you want to go. "Don't let your feet fall asleep," is what noted instructor Vic Braden tells his students.

THE FOREHAND GRIP—In executing a forehand stroke, use the Eastern forehand grip. This grip enables the palm of your hitting hand and the face of your racket to move on the same plane. This means that however you position your palm, so the racket face will be positioned. If you want the racket face straight up and down, you simply

Your grip should be firm, but not tight.

position your palm straight up and down.

In taking the grip, hold the throat of the racket in your left hand, keeping the head vertical. The handle end should be pointing at your belly.

Now shake hands with the racket handle with your right hand, placing your palm flat against the handle on the right side.

Don't bunch your fingers together. Keep them comfortably apart. You may want to extend your forefinger along the handle for added control. But do this only if it feels comfortable.

As you await the ball, you should be ready to move right or left, forward or back.

As you step to hit, your body shifts sideways to the net.

To check the grip, hold the racket away from your body and look to see that your palm and the face of the racket are on the same plane. When the palm is straight up and down, the racket face should also be straight up and down.

THE FOREHAND STROKE—Hitting a forehand

Keep a firm wrist.

drive in tennis and hitting a pitched baseball or softball are similar. Recall how you swing at a baseball. Take your left hand off the bat as you swing and you have the forehand stroke in tennis.

Let's say you're in the ready position, awaiting the ball's return. When you see the ball is coming

23

Turn your shoulders and hips; lean into the shot.

to your right, draw your right shoulder back, away from the net. The right foot swings back, too. Now your body is sideways to the net. Your weight is on your right foot. Your knees are slightly bent.

As the ball gets closer, start the racket forward. Keep the racket face perpendicular to the ground. Turn your shoulders and hips, leaning into the shot. If the ball is low, bend your knees more to get lower; don't merely lower the racket head.

Your weight shifts from your rear foot to your front foot as you swing. Hit through the ball; try to keep the ball on the strings for a split second.

Finish with a smooth follow-through. Your hitting arm should be reaching toward the sky and on a line with your target. Your wrist is still firm. The heel of the rear foot comes off the court surface.

As you move to make contact, be sure to watch the ball. In fact, try to watch the seams rotating as the ball approaches or try to read the manufacturer's name. You won't actually be able to

24

As you swing through, your weight shifts to your front foot. Finish with a high follow-through.

do this, but *trying* to do it will encourage you to concentrate more. Keep watching as the racket head makes contact with the ball. The beginner often worries about where the ball is going to go, and as a result jerks his or her head around to watch its flight. Don't allow yourself to do this. Keep your head steady. If you pull up before making contact, the shot you'll see will be a bad one.

Some beginners are frustrated by tennis because they never seem to have any idea of where their shots are going to go. They spray them to the right or left, long and short—all over the place. If this is happening to you, the problem may be with your wrist. Your wrist is flopping forward or back before you make contact. You must hit with a firm wrist, and with the racket face perfectly vertical at the moment of contact.

Try this: Stand sideways to a tall fence, positioning the racket as if you were about to hit a forehand. Hold the racket face against the fence at slightly higher than waist level. This is how the racket face and your wrist should be positioned when you make contact with the ball. Freeze this image in your mind. Anytime you seem unsure of how the racket face and your wrist should be positioned at the moment of impact, go back to the fence and place the racket head there.

ACHIEVING TOPSPIN—Topspin, also called

26

This is how your racket and wrist should be positioned in the forehand stroke as the racket makes contact with the ball.

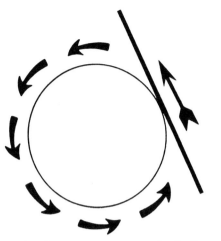

When the racket face comes up over the ball, topspin is the result. This view is from the side at the end of the stroke.

overspin or forward spin, causes the ball to veer downward after it is hit. The ball traces an arc that has a rainbow shape as it crosses the net. Then it bounces high. Topspin enables you to hit really hard groundstrokes without driving them beyond the base line.

To get topspin on the ball, keep the racket face vertical as you swing through. But start the racket low and sweep it forward on a low-to-high path. The racket face then brushes against the ball, lifting it and spinning it.

Some of your friends may tell you to "roll your wrist" to get topspin on the ball. That's not good advice. You want your wrist to be firm as you make contact. A stroke that travels on a low-to-high plane is the "secret" for achieving topspin.

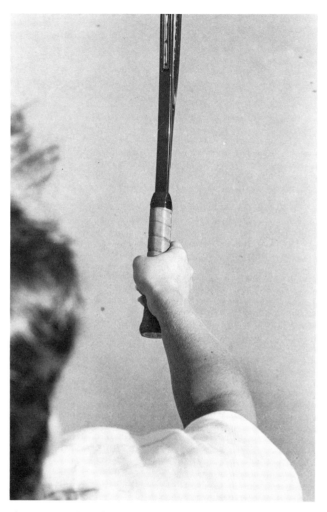

The Eastern backhand grip.

THE BACKHAND

The backhand drive is a stroke that's executed with the back of your hitting hand facing the net. It involves somewhat the same hand action you use when dealing cards.

The backhand drive is not difficult to learn because it's a natural stroke, more natural than the forehand drive. The hitting arm moves forward smoothly and easily; the body is out of the way.

The backhand drive and forehand drive have many similarities. You must, on both, get the racket head lower than the ball as you move to hit, then swing on a low-to-high plane. You must also have the racket face vertical as you make contact. Stroking in this manner enables you to put topspin on the ball.

THE GRIP—To hit a really effective backhand, you have to switch to what's called the Eastern backhand grip. Take the Eastern forehand grip first, your palm resting against the right side of the racket handle. Now move your hand one quarter of a turn to the right. This brings your palm to the top of the handle. Your thumb will be pointing downward along the left side of the handle.

Experienced players are often able to switch from the Eastern forehand to Eastern backhand and back again simply by twirling the handle in their hitting hand. This may be difficult for you

Thumb points downward along handle's left side.

to do, however. So use both hands. Hold the racket in your left hand as you turn the right hand on the handle.

THE STROKE—Begin from the ready position. When you realize that you're going to be taking the ball on your left side, switch to the backhand grip.

Swing your shoulders to your left, moving the racket into the backswing. Your elbow should bend only slightly. Step toward the right sideline with your right foot, bringing your body sideways

Step with your right foot to bring your body sideways to the net.

29

Shift your weight to your front foot as you swing . . .

... finish with a high follow-through.

to the net. Bend in the knees to get the racket head low. Remember, you're going to swing forward and up.

Sweep the racket forward, shifting your weight from your rear foot to your front. Your eyes are glued on the ball. Make contact in the center of the strings and with the ball well away from your body. Your wrist should be firm as you hit.

The racket keeps rising as you enter the follow-through phase of the stroke. At the end, your back heel is off the ground and your arms are fully extended and reaching for the sky.

THE TWO-HANDED BACKHAND—Some players lack the strength to hit a forceful backhand one-handed. The solution is to use the two-handed backhand. Not only will the two-handed backhand enable you to get more punch into the stroke, it also encourages you to hit with a firm wrist. In other words, it's a teaching tool.

The chief criticism of the two-handed backhand is that it reduces your reach. The reduction is only slight, however. And this drawback is out-weighed by your increased ability to get the ball over the net with power and accuracy.

If you're right-handed, your right hand should be the bottom hand as you grip the racket. Use the Eastern backhand grip with the right hand. With your left hand, use the Eastern forehand grip.

As the ball comes toward you, start turning

The two-handed backhand.

Don't slap the ball . . .

. . . **swing through it.**

sideways to the net. Draw the racket back, looking over your shoulder at the ball.

Bend in the knees, lowering the racket head. Shift your weight from your rear foot to your front foot as you swing through.

Don't slap the ball. Swing through it. As you follow through, your arms should reach for the sky.

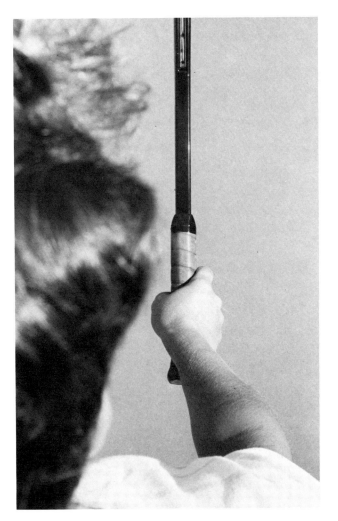

THE SERVE

The serve is the most important stroke in tennis. It is the only stroke that gives you complete control over the way in which the ball will be hit. With all others, you're merely returning a ball hit by your opponent. You may have to run and get it. You never know at what height it's going to arrive. But with the serve, you toss the ball up to exactly where you want it, and then hit away.

In the early days of tennis, the serve was used merely as a method of putting the ball in play. But more and more it came to be looked upon as an offensive weapon. This doesn't mean, however, that you should be trying to hammer every serve as hard as you can in an effort to score a quick point. Instead, you should use the serve to put your opponent on the defensive. You can hit the serve deep, you can hit it away from your opponent, or you can hit it to his or her weakest side. There's nothing better than an accurate, smartly hit serve.

THE GRIP—For serving, use a grip that's halfway between the Eastern forehand and Eastern backhand grips. It's called the Continental grip.

The Continental grip is halfway between the Eastern forehand and Eastern backhand.

First, take the Eastern forehand grip, then rotate the palm one-eighth of a turn to the right.

THE STANCE—When you serve, your target will usually be the corner of the court on your opponent's backhand side. This is likely to be the opponent's weakest side. You want to present yourself with the best hitting target. This means that when you're serving from the right side—the "deuce court," as it's called—you should position yourself as close as possible to the center mark. When serving from the left side—the "ad court"—position yourself about three steps from the mark.

The toes of your left foot should be about an inch behind the base line. When you're serving from the deuce court, your front shoulder should point toward the left net post. When serving from the ad court, your front shoulder should point toward the right net post.

In either case, keep your feet a shoulder-width apart. Hold the racket at belt level.

THE TOSS—The action of the serve involves two distinct actions. First, you toss the ball. Second, you swing. If either isn't right, the serve won't be right. Pay as much attention to achieving a good toss as you do toward developing an accurate, power-filled stroke.

The average beginner wants to toss the ball up in front of the body. But a toss of this type makes for an unnatural stroke. Instead, you should toss the ball up to the right of your head and as far out in front of your body as possible.

As for height, the ball should climb to about a racket's length above your upstretched tossing hand. This type of toss puts the ball out in front of your body, meaning you can get your forearm and wrist into the shot, which helps achieve power.

Hold the ball lightly on the fingertips of your left hand as you get set to toss. Use your entire arm to make the toss, not merely your hand and wrist. Watch the ball go up. Release it at about eye level. Allow the arm to keep moving in a follow-through. The ball should always go straight up, just as if it were rising inside a pipe.

Beginners often like to toss the ball very high, then smack it when it falls back into the racket's hitting zone. This involves a wait, which disrupts the flow of your swing. The better way is to hit the ball at the top of its rise, before it starts falling.

Keep in mind that you don't have to hit a bad toss, that is, there's never any penalty. Just let the ball drop. Then toss it and hit again.

THE STROKE—In international competition, Americans have traditionally been noted for their powerful serves. According to one theory, this is

Use your entire arm to make the toss, not merely your hand and wrist. The ball should climb to about a racket's length above your upstretched hand.

because the arm action in serving is similar to throwing, and the most popular American sports—baseball, football, and basketball—all involve throwing to a very high degree. In most other countries, a kicking game—soccer—is more popular than any other.

Think of the serving stroke as being similar to the way a pitcher throws a baseball. In the midst of his windup, the pitcher shows most of his back to the batter, then turns his shoulders and lower body as he whips the ball to the plate. The same type of body turn is a critical part of the serve in tennis.

As your left hand tosses the ball up, your weight shifts to your rear foot, and at the same time you loop the racket behind your shoulder.

As the ball goes up, loop the racket behind your shoulder. Sweep the racket forward as the ball reaches its peak.

As the ball reaches its peak, bring the racket upward and forward, shifting your weight to your front foot. Keep your chin up. Keep your eyes on the ball.

As you follow through, your back foot steps onto the court. The racket head ends up on the left side of your body.

In order to get the ball over the net consistently, you must remember always to swing up and out. Many players want to hit the serve down. But even if you're much taller than average, you'll put the ball into the net by hitting down. Even taller-than-average adults must hit up and out.

SERVING WITH SPIN—By putting spin on the ball, you can slam the ball hard and still put it within the court. But don't try using spin until you become skilled in serving and want to improve.

There is, for instance, the topspin serve. In this, the racket face, moving on a low-to-high path, comes up over the ball, causing it to veer downward and bounce high.

There is also the slice serve. In this, the racket face contacts the side of the ball while moving from inside to outside. In the case of a right-

Your weight shifts forward as the racket swings through; step out onto the court.

handed server, the slice serve kicks—bounces abruptly—to the right.

The slice serve is a good weapon to have. It is especially valuable if you happen to be a left-hander, for it kicks naturally to a right-hander's backhand.

You'll also hear about the American twist. You get an American twist by lifting the racket face upward at the moment of impact. This causes the ball to rotate forward, resulting in a very high kick.

Beware of the American twist, however. It places a tremendous strain on the server's back and elbow and can lead to serious elbow damage.

THE SECOND SERVE—Another tactical advantage of the serve, besides putting you in control of the ball, is that you get two chances to get the ball in. If the first is missed, it's called a fault, and you serve again. If the second serve is missed, it's a double fault—and you lose the point. The score is 0-15.

If your first serve fails to land in your opponent's service court, try to figure out what went wrong and correct it. Let's say you put the ball into the net. This could be the result of a poor toss. The ball was too far out in front of you when you hit.

If the ball goes out to the right or left, check the positioning of your feet. The ball often travels in the same direction as the toes are pointing.

When it comes to making the second serve, always use the same swing you use on your first serve. Don't swing softly. A pitty-pat serve gives your opponent a tremendous advantage.

A topspin serve will help you to make your second serve very effective. Suppose your first (topspin) serve is long. On the second serve, you'll want to increase the spin on the ball, causing it to drop sooner. This means you must swing harder. This increases the ball's spin, bringing it down faster.

THE VOLLEY

Up to this point, the shots this book has discussed have all been groundstrokes; they're shots in which the ball has been hit after it bounced. The volley is different. It's a shot that's hit before the ball bounces.

When you volley, your opponent has less time to get into position for the return. The volley frequently ends the point outright.

APPROACHING THE NET—Hit your volleys from as close to the net as possible. How do you get to the net? Let's say you've hit a deep groundstroke. A weak return is the result. Your strategy should be to dart forward and hit the ball to a deep base line corner, making contact at about the service line. This is called an approach shot. When it's well placed, it's your ticket to the net. If your opponent manages to return the approach shot, you then volley the return.

The key to a successful approach is anticipating what your opponent is going to do and then reacting accordingly. You want to start moving even before the opponent contacts the ball. Most beginners fail to do this. They don't start moving until the ball is on its way. That's defensive tennis.

To be aggressive, to take the net and volley, you must decide in advance what your opponent is going to do, and then either break for the net or stay back.

Watch your opponent's swing as he or she moves to hit. If the opponent's racket face drops below the level of the ball and he or she angles the face back, you can be pretty sure the return is going to go high and deep—and you should remain at the base line. But if the racket face is positioned at about the same level as the ball, the shot is almost surely going to be a drive.

When it's a drive, start moving forward before the ball strikes the racket. Take two steps toward the net, see where the ball is going, and then step in that direction. You'll either move diagonally or toward the net. If you go toward the net, remember that the closer you can get to the net the better.

THE VOLLEY STROKE—Hit the volley from the forehand or backhand side. In either case, use the Eastern backhand grip. This gives you the firm grip you expect on the backhand; it's also effective for hitting the forehand volley because of the way the stroke is executed.

The volley stroke is a short, punching stroke, something like a jab in boxing. As the ball comes toward you, turn your shoulders to bring the racket back. Move crisply as you swing. Keep your wrist firm. Shift your weight forward and lean into the shot.

The volley is hit with a short, punching stroke; there's little follow-through.

For the backhand volley, you must contact the ball farther out in front of your body than when hitting from a forehand volley. This time, of course, you pivot in the other direction. Lean

into the shot as you bring the racket forward. Again, there's not much backswing and not much follow-through.

When you have to volley the ball from below the level of the net tape, get down low by bending your knees. It's a mistake to try to get the ball by merely lowering the racket head. Your entire body must go down.

On the backhand side, the stroke is the same—short and crisp.

For the half volley, bend your front knee and get down low. Keep your forearm parallel to the court.

Whenever you volley, try to hit the ball deep. The best volley is one that's hit on a diagonal path. That kind of shot either wins the point or forces your opponent far out of position. But the angled volley is not easy to execute. As a begin-ner, simply try to keep the ball deep and in play. Once you've become experienced with this tactic, you can start trying to angle your volleys.

THE HALF VOLLEY—As some instructors point out, this shot is poorly named; a better name would be the half groundstroke. It's a stroke in which the ball is hit almost immediately after it bounces.

It's not a stroke you usually plan to hit. It's hit out of necessity. For example, it's often the stroke you call upon when you get caught in the midcourt area with the ball coming toward your feet.

You can hit the half volley from either the forehand or backhand side. Get down low by bending your knees. You should bend your knees so deeply, in fact, that you lower your hitting hand and arm to the level of the ball. The racket handle and your forearm should be about parallel with the court as you stroke. Keep the swing as compact as possible.

The overhead stroke is like a serve with a short backswing. As you bring the racket forward, shift your weight to your front foot.

THE OVERHEAD

The overhead, sometimes called the overhead smash or, simply, smash, is a stroke in which you slam the ball hard and deep. It is often the response to an opponent's lob, a ball meant to go high—over your head, in fact—and very deep.

When hit properly, the overhead is almost always a winner. The opponent simply can't get to the ball. Even if the opponent does, the speed

45

Your arm straightens as you make contact with the ball.
Be sure to follow through.

and power of the shot usually forces an error.

GETTING IN POSITION—Before you begin your backswing, get in position. In fact, getting in position *early* is a must. Watch closely as your opponent gets set to swing. Watch how the racket face is positioned. When you see a lob coming (and you're close to the net), start backpedaling immediately or turn and run back like an outfielder chasing a fly ball. Get your feet in position, your body turned, the racket back.

Try to hit your overheads before the ball bounces. Doing so means that your opponent has to be lightning fast to get into position to hit a return. When you allow the ball to bounce, you give your opponent more time. Of course, sometimes the lob is going to be dropping toward you at such a steep angle that hitting it before it bounces will be very difficult. A ball that lands very deep can also be a problem. Hit such balls after they bounce.

But whether you hit the ball before or after it bounces, always try to hit it deep. If you drill your overheads to within a few feet of the base line, seldom will you have a return to worry about.

THE OVERHEAD STROKE—The stroking action you use is the same as when you serve. Use the serving grip, the Continental grip.

One important difference between the overhead and the serve is that you use a shorter backswing for the overhead. Some instructors compare the overhead stroke to the arm action you use in hammering a nail into the wall above your head. You wouldn't take a full backswing with the hammer. If you did, you'd have trouble hitting the target squarely. The same is true of the overhead stroke. Keep a lid on your backswing. This gives you more time to get ready to hit a ball that is falling faster and from a greater height than your service toss.

THE LOB

The lob is a groundstroke that is lofted high into the air over your opponent's upstretched racket. Use the lob to force an aggressive opponent away from the net or earn yourself time to get in position for the next shot. You can call on the lob anytime during a point.

You don't have to learn a new grip and stroke to be able to lob. Use the Eastern forehand grip and the forehand stroke. The difference is that you tilt back the racket's face as you swing through. This is what sends the ball high into the air.

Your swing has to be smooth and controlled from beginning to end. Bend your front knee as you move in to hit.

The idea is to get the racket face under the ball. Swing on an upward plane. Keep a firm grip. At the end of the follow-through, the racket should be about head high or a bit higher.

Always hit the lob deep. A lob that fails to go deep gives your opponent the opportunity for an overhead smash. In practice sessions and whenever you warm up for a game, practice lobbing the ball to within four or five feet of the base line.

Tilt back the racket face as you move to hit; get under the ball.

The best place to aim the lob is over the left shoulder of your opponent at the net. He or she must then race back to the left to get the ball. Trying to return a ball that is hit high and to one's left, or backhand, side is no easy matter.

The racket should end up head high or higher.

Above and facing page: The drop shot is a gentle stroke that causes the ball to "drop" . . .

. . . just beyond the net.

THE DROP SHOT

Suppose you're competing against an opponent who is slow to react, doesn't move very fast, or is tiring. The drop shot is a good weapon to use. Hit with a delicate touch from the front part of the court, the ball "drops" just over the net with little or no forward bounce. The drop shot is especially effective on clay courts.

When hitting a drop shot, use the same grip and backswing you use for a forehand drive. But the forward swing is much different. With the drop shot, the idea is to stroke softly and put underspin (also called backspin) on the ball.

Tilt back the racket's face, then swing through on a low-to-high plane. It's a slower, more deliberate swing than the standard forehand swing. There's virtually no follow-through.

A drop shot should be hit from your own forecourt. Attempting a drop shot from your backcourt is an invitation to disaster. Your opponent will have all the time in the world to get into position to slam it back.

There's also the drop volley, a drop shot that is hit before the ball bounces. Like the drop shot itself, the drop volley requires delicacy. It's also called the "stop" volley. Its success depends not only on the proper angling of the racket head but also in relaxing your grip just before you make

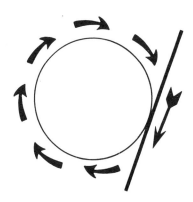

When the racket face moves downward in this fashion (as seen from the side), underspin is the result.

contact. This deadens the flight of the ball, causing it to drop from the racket into the opponent's court.

The serve is on its way. Is it coming to your backhand or forehand?

RETURNING THE SERVE

Tennis instructors agree that the serve is the game's most important shot. The second most important is the service return. If you're unable to return or serve consistently, there are times when you're going to be beaten by a skilled server on the basis of his or her service stroke alone.

When waiting for the serve, use the Eastern forehand grip. Switch to the Eastern backhand if the ball comes to your left.

Take your stance in front of the base line. When receiving on the right (or deuce) court, its usually best to stand fairly close to the right sideline. Of course, if your opponent is capable of serving the ball wide, move closer to the center mark.

The same holds true when receiving in the left (or ad) court. Position yourself fairly close to the sideline but be prepared to adjust toward the center mark, depending on the serving capabilities of your opponent.

When you watch a professional match on television, note how each player adjusts his or her starting position. No one, for example, who was about to receive John McEnroe's booming slice serve in the deuce court would think of standing close to the right sideline. The ball would spurt right by.

As you're getting set to receive the serve, watch the server's racket carefully. Try to tell in advance whether the ball is coming to your forehand or backhand. When you decide, say to yourself, "forehand" or "backhand." You should be moving toward the ball before it bounces.

If your opponent has a really powerful serve, don't try to return it with your regular forehand. Your stroke should be more of a blocking stroke. Position the racket so it's almost vertical at impact. Keep your wrist firm. Your forward motion as you move to make contact plus the speed of the ball as it rebounds will generate plenty of power.

If your opponent stays at the base line after serving, hit your return deep. Don't give the player the opportunity to get to the net.

If the server does rush in, lob or try a passing shot down the line or cross-court.

If the opponent's second serve is weak, move in on it. Try to drill your return into one of the corners.

TENNIS TACTICS

As a beginner, your game plan in any given match is simple: keep the ball in play. Don't try to be fancy. More points are lost by making errors than through the shot-making ability of one's opponent. Concentrate on getting the ball back over the net. The points will come.

Whenever you can, hit the ball deep and down the middle. Hitting down the middle keeps your opponent from returning the ball on a sharp angle. It'll thus be easier for you to return.

And keep in mind that the net is six inches lower at the middle than at the side posts. This means there's a greater chance of the ball clearing the net at the middle.

Once you've become consistent in hitting the ball down the middle and deep, you can start trying to be more aggressive. This means going to the net whenever you get the opportunity, and volleying quickly and sharply.

Before you attempt to become a net player, however, you must have sound groundstrokes and a hard and accurate serve. You also have to have a strong volley. There's no use in going to the net unless you're a sharp volleyer.

CONCENTRATING—When you're involved in a match, don't let yourself be distracted by people playing on the next court, a decision made by one official or another, the spectators, the score,

From beginning to end, keep your eyes glued on the ball.

or the antics of your opponent. Your only concern should be the shot and how you're going to play it.

Don't worry about the ball you've just hit badly

or failed to hit. Don't be thinking ahead as to how you're going to hit your opponent's return. Smart players concentrate only on the shot they're hitting.

From the standpoint of tactics, there is nothing more important than keeping your eye on the ball. "The court isn't moving," says instructor Lloyd Lifton, "the ball is. *Look* at the ball—not at where it's been or where it's going."

ATTACKING WEAKNESSES—After a few points, or even as you warm up, you should be able to figure out the weak points of your opponent's game. Let's say that his or her backhand is one of them. Keep hitting shots to it until the opponent flubs one. Hit wide to the opponent's forehand, then wide to his or her backhand. Having to hit the shot on the run will make it more difficult. Also try hitting the ball deep to the opponent's backhand and then going to the net. Use the same tactic if your opponent has a weak forehand.

When you're facing a player whose ground-strokes usually fall short, play in closer to the service line. Punch your shots into the corners, making your opponent run. Be ready to dart to the net.

If your opponent seems reluctant to come to the net, draw the player in with short shots, then lob. Or try to pass the opponent with a shot down the line.

When your opponent is not in good condition and slow-moving on the court, aim your shots first into one corner and then the other. Bring the player in with a drop shot and then force him or her back with a lob. Make the player move constantly.

GENERAL STRATEGY—"Never change a winning game" is a piece of advice you'll often hear. If you've built up a lead by staying back and pounding your opponent's forehand, stay with that strategy. Don't—for some unknown reason—start rushing the net.

Another rule is "Always change a losing game." If your base line strokes are getting you nowhere, try going to the net more. If you have been going in, and you have little to show for it, try staying back more.

COPING WITH DIFFERENT COURT SURFACES—If you learn to play tennis on clay courts and then switch to another surface—concrete, for instance—you are likely to have problems. Clay is considered a "slow" surface. The ball bounces higher and sometimes unevenly. You slide. On concrete, which is "fast," everything is speeded up. The ball zips in and stays relatively low. Sometimes it skids.

When you move from one surface to another, your timing goes awry. You may misplay one ball after another. The only solution is to change your style of play.

Clay is a slow surface. Cement and wood are

fast. (Grass is fast, too, but grass courts are rare today.) When it comes to synthetic surfaces, it's more difficult to make general statements. Some are fast, others are slow, and still others are in-between. Asphalt also ranks in between fast and slow.

Hit a few balls on any new court to get the "feel" of it. If you're going from a fast or medium-fast surface to a slow surface, you'll find you're often stretching forward in an effort to hit the ball. Even then, you barely get your racket on it before it bounces a second time.

Adjust by moving forward for every ball. Shorten your backswing so you're able to keep a smooth stroke. If the court has some rough spots, watch for bad bounces. Keep alert, ready to dart to the right or left in coping with the ball's erratic behavior. You may also have to change the direction of your stroke at the last second. Try to meet the ball on the fly as often as you can when playing on a bad surface.

Moving from a slow to fast surface is even more difficult. The ball comes at you so fast you're never really ready to hit it. When you do manage to get your racket on the ball, you're "late." Forehands go off the court to your right, while backhands fly in the other direction.

You have to move faster and get in position

On clay, a "slow" surface, watch for tricky bounces.

Enjoy yourself; tennis should
always be fun.

58

sooner. Try to get to the spot where the ball is going before it gets there.

Shorten your swing and start it earlier. Try hitting more cross-court shots. It will be hard for you to hit a cross-court out.

In terms of strategy, be patient on a slow court. There's no need to take chances. Play steady tennis.

The fast court rewards the power hitter. Whenever you have a chance to put the ball away, do so. And don't hesitate to go to the net.

A writer for *World Tennis* magazine once asked John McEnroe this question: "If you could give one piece of advice to today's young player, what would it be?"

This was McEnroe's reply: "If I had to tell a kid one thing, it would be enjoy the game."

Always try to win, of course. That's what tennis is all about. But don't feel bad when you lose—as long as you played your best.

This doesn't mean that you should enjoy losing. But if you have to win in order to have fun, tennis is going to cause you a great many disappointments. After all, in every match there's always one loser; in every 64-player tournament, there are 63 boys or girls who fail to win.

When you do lose, learn from the experience. Go out and practice to overcome the weaknesses in your game.

With every match, you should seek to improve, even if it's only a tiny bit. If you can improve steadily, without worrying about wins and losses, you'll soon be winning many more matches than you lose.

GLOSSARY

ACE—A point earned by serving a ball that goes untouched by the opponent's racket.

AD—Short for advantage.

AD COURT—When serving or returning the serve, the left-hand court as you face the net.

ADVANTAGE—A point won by a player after deuce.

ALL—A scoring term meaning "for each" or "apiece," as in 15-all or 30-all.

ALLEY—The 4½-foot strip on each side of the court used in doubles play. The two doubles alleys increase the size of the court from a width of 27 feet in singles to 36 feet in doubles.

BACKCOURT—The area of the court between the base line and the service line.

BACKHAND—A stroke used by a right-hander to hit balls on his or her left side and by left-handers to hit strokes on the right side. The body pivots so as to turn the back side of the hitting hand toward the net.

BACKSPIN—*See* Underspin.

BACKSWING—The beginning part of the stroke. The hitting arm and racket go back to a position in which the downward or forward motion of the stroke begins.

BASE LINE—The back line at each end of the court.

BREAK—*See* Service Break

BREAK POINT—A situation (when the score is love-40, 15-40 or 30-40) in which the server is within one point of losing the game.

CENTER LINE—*See* Center Service Line.

CENTER MARK—The mark on the base line on each court that bisects the base line.

CENTER SERVICE LINE—The line on each side of the net (and perpendicular to it) that divides the service courts in half.

CONTINENTAL GRIP—*See* page 34

CROSS-COURT SHOT—A ball hit diagonally from one court over the net into the court opposite (rather than down-the-line or down-the-middle).

DEUCE—A scoring term that refers to a score of 40-40 (40-all) or any tied game score beyond that point.

DEUCE COURT—In serving or returning the serve, the right-hand court as you face the net.

DOUBLE FAULT—To lose a point by making two consecutive unsuccessful serves.

DOUBLES—A contest in which four players compete, two on each side.

DOWN-THE-LINE SHOT—A ball hit from near a sideline that travels parallel to it.

DROP SHOT—A groundstroke that is hit in such a way that it drops just beyond the net with little or no forward bounce.

DROP VOLLEY—A volley hit in such a way that it drops just beyond the net with no forward bounce.

EASTERN BACKHAND GRIP—*See* page 28

EASTERN FOREHAND GRIP—*See* page 20

ERROR—Any mistake that costs a player a point.

FACE—The hitting surface of the racket as formed by the intersecting strings.

FAULT—A service ball that fails to strike in the proper court. *See* Double Fault, Foot Fault.

FOLLOW-THROUGH—The finishing part of the stroke that occurs after the ball is struck.

FOOT FAULT—Illegal foot movement before or during a serve that causes the serve to be disallowed.

FOREHAND—The stroke used by right-handers to hit balls on their right and by left-handers to hit balls on their left.

GAME—A tennis contest that is complete when one player or side wins at least four points while holding at least a two-point lead over the opposition.

GROUNDSTOKE—A stroke used to hit the ball after it has bounced.

HALF VOLLEY—A stroke in which the ball is hit just after it has bounced.

HEAD—The oval-shaped part of the racket that holds the strings.

LOB—A groundstroke that is hit high and deep so as to pass over the outstretched racket of one's opponent.

LOB VOLLEY—A shot that is hit high and deep from a volleying position close to the net.

LOVE—A scoring term that refers to a player who has won no points in a game or no games in a set.

MATCH—A contest between two players or sides that is decided when one player or side wins a certain number of sets (usually two out of three).

MATCH POINT—The final point of a match.

MIDCOURT—The area on each side of the net near the service line.

NET—The mesh fabric strung across the middle of the court.

NET BALL—A shot that strikes the net and falls back on the same side as the hitter.

OVERHEAD—A forehand stroke that is hit while the ball is higher than one's head.

OVERHEAD SMASH—A very hard overhead.

POINT—The smallest unit of scoring. Four points win a game, providing the player or side has gained a lead of at least two points.

SERVE—The stroke that puts the ball in play on every point.

SERVICE BREAK—To win a game against an opponent's serve.

SERVICE COURT—The area in which the serve must land to be good. The court's center line divides the area between the service line on each side of the net into the right service court and left service court.

SERVICE RETURN—The stroke used to return a serve.

SET—A contest that is completed when one player or side wins at least six games while holding a two-game lead.

SET POINT—The point that decides the set.

SINGLES—A contest in which two players compete, one on each side of the net.

SMASH—*See* Overhead Smash.

TIE BREAKER—A method used to determine the outcome of a set when the score is 6-6 (6-all). There is both a 5-point-out-of-9 and a 7-point-out-of-12 tie break system.

TOPSPIN—Forward rotation of the ball which causes it to arc downward and bounce high.

UNDERSPIN—Reverse rotation on the ball; also called backspin. Underspin retards the ball's bounce.

VOLLEY—A shot in which the ball is hit before it bounces.

62

This Book
Belongs to